*The Autobiography of a Horse*
*by*
*Anna Sewell*

Adapted as an ELT Reader
Illustrated by Johanna Gousset

# Before reading

## About Anna Sewell

1. **Read and circle.**
   **Guess the answers.**

Anna Sewell lived in England from 1820 to 1878. She loved [1]dogs / horses. Her grandparents had a farm and Anna learnt to ride a horse. Sadly, she hurt her [2]knees / ankles in a fall when she was fourteen years old. After that, she was unable to walk and she learnt to [3]drive a horse and carriage / ride a bike.

Anna's mother was a/an [4]author / teacher. She wrote [5]plays / children's books. Anna helped her mother to edit the books.

In those days, people [6]treated / did not treat horses very well and this upset Anna. She decided to write a book about horses, and she wrote *Black Beauty* between 1870 and 1877. Sadly, she died just [7]before / after it was published, so she never saw how popular it was.

The story is told by the horse and not by a person. This helps the reader to understand how horses feel. The book was very successful, and it helped to stop [8]cruelty to / deaths of horses.

## Look at the pictures in the book.

**1. Answer the question and tick (✓).**

**1.** Who do you think the main characters in the book are?

**a)** horses ☐      **b)** people ☐      **c)** dogs ☐

**2. Label the pictures with words from the box.**

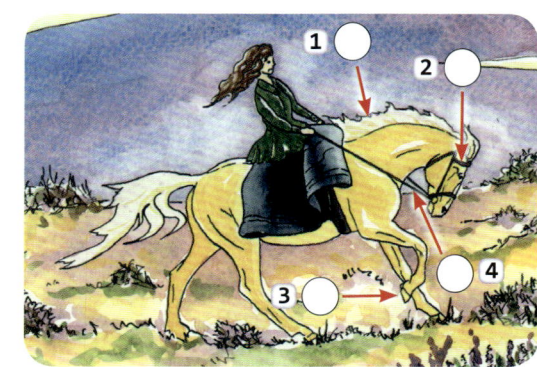

a. mane
b. hoof
c. reins
d. bridle

**3. Find these things and write the page number.**

**1.** field ( )    **2.** carriage ( )    **3.** hare ( )

**4.** stable ( )    **5.** saddle ( )    **6.** whip ( )

**7.** pony ( )    **8.** stream ( )

# Chapter 1
## My Early Home

The first place I can remember was a lovely green field with a beautiful *pond. There were some trees by it, and *water-lilies grew at the deep end. I lived there with my mother.

In the daytime, I ran by her side, and at night I lay down close by her. When it was hot, we used to stand by the pond in the *shade of the trees, and when it was cold, we had a nice warm *stable.

As soon as I was old enough to eat grass, my mother used to go out to work in the daytime, and come back in the evening.

There were six young *foals in the field besides me. They were older than I was. We had great fun. We used to *gallop round the field together. Sometimes they kicked and bit each other.

shade: coolness and darkness away from sunlight
stable: the building that horses live in
foal: a young horse
gallop: to run (horses)

pond

waterlily

One day, my mother *neighed to me to come to her, and she told me, 'You mustn't kick and bite. I want you to grow up gentle and good, and not learn bad ways.'

I have never forgotten my mother's advice. I knew that she was a wise old horse, and that our master loved her. He called her Duchess.

Our master was a good, kind man. He gave us good food, a good home and kind words.

We were all *fond of him, and my mother loved him very much. When she saw him at the gate, she neighed happily, and *trotted up to him. He *patted and *stroked her and said, 'Hello, Duchess, and how is your little Blackie?'

I was black, so he called me Blackie. Sometimes, he gave me a piece of bread, which was very good, and sometimes he brought a carrot for my mother. All the horses came to him, but I think we were his favourites.

neigh: (horses) to call or talk
be fond of: to like
trot: to move faster than a walk (horses)
pat: to touch gently with your hand
to show affection
stroke: to run your hand across
an animal's fur to show affection

# Chapter 2
## The Hunt

Before I was two years old something happened, which I have never forgotten. It was early in the spring, and it was *misty.

We were in the lower part of the field when we heard loud cries. The oldest foal raised his head and said, 'That's the dogs!'

Then, he immediately galloped off to the upper part of the field, and we followed. There, we could look over the *hedge and see several fields. My mother was also standing there.

misty: a little foggy
hedge: a wall made by bushes

And soon the dogs ran across the field next to ours. They barked very loudly.

'They've found a *hare,' said my mother, 'and if they come this way, we'll see the *hunt.'

A number of men **on horseback** came after them, some of them in green coats, all galloping as fast as they could.

Then, the dogs ran towards our field.

> hare: a very large rabbit with long back legs
>
> hunt: a chase to kill a wild animal

'Now we'll see the hare,' said my mother;
and just then a frightened hare ran by.
The dogs chased after it. It was *horrible.
They *leapt over the stream, and ran across
the field followed by the huntsmen. Six or eight
men on horseback jumped over the stream after
them.

on horseback: riding a horse
horrible: not nice, very bad
leap: to jump

I watched them for a while, then when I looked back at the stream, there was a sad sight. I saw two beautiful horses on the ground. One was in the stream, *struggling to get up, and the other was *groaning on the grass. One of the riders was getting out of the water covered with *mud, the other lay very still on the ground.

'The man's neck is broken,' said my mother.

We stood and looked on. Many of the riders were with the young man. My master was with him too.

There was **no** noise now. Even the dogs were quiet. They seemed to know that something was wrong.

They carried the young man to our master's house. I heard afterwards that it was George Gordon, the *squire's only son and that he died that day.

struggle: to try very hard to do something
groan: to make a loud noise when you are in pain or upset
mud: earth and water
squire: a man who owns land and a large house in the countryside

People rode off in all directions to the doctor's, to the vet's, and to Squire Gordon's.

Mr Bond, the vet, came to look at the black horse. It lay groaning on the grass. He felt him all over, and shook his head. 'One of his legs is broken,' said the vet. 'There's nothing I can do. He's in too much pain. I'll have to *shoot him.'

Then, someone ran to our master's house and came back with a gun. There was a loud bang and a horrible cry, and then there was silence. The black horse moved no more.

My mother was very *upset. 'I've known that horse for years,' she said. 'His name was Rob Roy. He was a good horse.'

She never went to that part of the field again after that.

shoot: to kill with a gun
upset: very sad

# Chapter 3
# My Breaking In

I was now beginning to grow handsome. My coat was fine and soft, and it was bright black. I had one white foot and a pretty white star on my forehead.

My master did not want to sell me until I was four years old. 'Teenagers shouldn't work like men, and foals shouldn't work like horses,' he said.

When I was four years old, Squire Gordon came to look at me. He examined my eyes, my mouth, and my legs. Then, I had to walk and trot and gallop for him.

He seemed to like me, and said, 'When you have *broken him in, I'd like to buy him.'

My master said, 'I'll break him in myself. I don't want him to be frightened or hurt.'

He began the next day.

> break (a horse) in: to train a horse to be ridden and to pull a vehicle

Not everyone will know what 'breaking in' is, so I will describe it to you. It means to teach a horse to wear a *saddle and *bridle, and to carry a man, woman or child on his back and to go the way they wish, and to go quietly.

The horse also needs to have a cart fixed behind it, so that it cannot walk or trot without *dragging the cart. Then, it must go fast or slow, just as its driver wishes. It must never jump at something it sees, or speak to other horses, or bite, or kick.

Now I was to have a *bit and bridle.

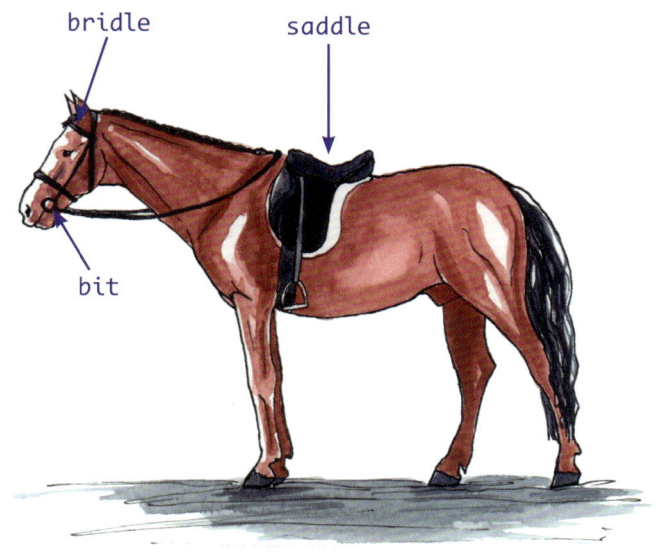

bridle                    saddle

bit

drag: to pull something heavy
that is hard to pull

It won't have any *will of its own. It will always do its master's will, even though it may be very tired or hungry.

My master gave me some oats as usual, and then, he got the bit into my mouth, and the bridle fixed, but it was a *nasty thing! A big piece of cold, hard metal is pushed into your mouth, between your teeth, and over your tongue. **I hated it!** But I knew my mother always wore one when she went out, and all horses did when they were *grown up. And so, with the nice oats, and with my master's kind words, I began to wear my bit and bridle.

Next came the saddle, but that was not so bad. My master put it on my back very gently, while the stable boy held my head. He patted me and talked to me all the time.

Then, I had a few oats, then a little leading about. He did this every day until I began to look for the oats and the saddle.

At last, one morning, my master got on my back and rode me round the field. It felt strange, but I felt quite proud to carry my master.

will: control or being allowed to make decisions yourself and to do what you want
nasty: not nice
grown up: an adult

He continued to ride me a little every day, and I soon became used to it.

The next unpleasant business was putting on the iron shoes. That was very hard at first. My master went with me to the *blacksmith's *forge, to see that I was not hurt or frightened.

The blacksmith took my feet in his hand, one after the other, and cut away some of the *hoof. It did not hurt me, so I stood still on three legs till he finished.

Then, he took a piece of iron the shape of my foot, and put it on. He put some *nails through the shoe into my hoof, so that the shoe was firmly on. My feet felt very *stiff and heavy, but in time I got used to it.

I must not forget to mention one part of my training, which I thought was very good. My master sent me for a fortnight to a farmer. His farm had a field next to the railway. There were some sheep and cows in the field.

blacksmith: a person who makes and repairs things in iron
forge: the place where a blacksmith works
hoof: a horse's foot
nail: a hard metal pin
stiff: hard, doesn't change shape

I shall never forget the first train that ran by. I was eating quietly in the field by the railway, when I heard a strange sound in the distance. Then suddenly, a long, black, noisy train flew by.

I turned and galloped to the far side of the field as fast as I could. There I stood *snorting with fear.

snort: (horses) to make a noise when it is excited or frightened

That day many other trains went by, some more
slowly. These stopped at the station, and they
sometimes made an *awful *shriek and groan.
I thought it was terrible, but the cows went
on eating very quietly. They didn't raise their
heads as the noisy, black thing went past.

For the first few days, I was frightened.
Then, when I knew that this terrible creature
never came into the field, I began to ignore it,
like the cows and the sheep did.

awful: very bad
shriek: a loud cry

Since then, I have seen many horses upset and frightened by a train. But thanks to my good master's care, I am not frightened at railway stations.

Now if anyone wants to break in a young horse well, that is the way.

My master often took me out with my mother, because she could teach me better than a strange horse.

'The better you *behave, the better you will be *treated,' she told me. 'But,' she said, 'there are a lot of different kinds of men; there are good, thoughtful men like our master, and there are bad, cruel men, who shouldn't own a horse or a dog. I hope you will have a good master; but a horse never knows who will buy him. It is luck. But still you must always do your best.'

> behave: to act or to do things in a certain way
> treat: to speak and act towards

# Chapter 4
# Birtwick Park

It was early in May, when a man came from Squire Gordon's to take me to the hall.

My master said, 'Goodbye, Blackie. Be a good horse, and always do your best.'

I could not say goodbye, so I put my nose into his hand. He patted me kindly, and I left my first home.

As I lived for a few years with Squire Gordon, I will tell you something about the place.

Squire Gordon's park was outside the village of Birtwick. It was entered by a large gate. A long drive brought you to the house and the gardens. Beyond this, there was the *paddock, the old *orchard, and the stables.

paddock: a field where horses are kept
orchard: a field where fruit trees are grown

The stable which I was taken to was very big, with four good *stalls.

The *groom put me in a lovely, clean stall. I could see all that went on.

He gave me some very nice oats, he patted me, spoke kindly, and then went away.

I looked round. In the stall next to mine, stood a little fat, grey pony, with a thick *mane and tail. He had a very pretty head, and a little nose.

I put my head over the door of my stall, and said, 'Hello. What's your name?'

He turned round and said, 'My name's Merrylegs. I carry the two little girls on my back. They love me, and so does Joe. Joe's the stable boy. Are you going to live next door to me in that stall?'

I said, 'Yes.'

'Well, then,' he said, 'I hope you're *good-tempered. I don't like anyone next door who bites.'

Just then a horse's head looked over from the next stall. She was a tall chestnut *mare, with a long neck. She looked *cross.

'So, they've given you my stall,' she said. 'It's strange for a foal like you to come and throw a lady out of her own home.'

groom: a man who looks after horses
mane: horse's hair
good-tempered: nice
mare: a female horse
cross: a bit angry

'I'm sorry,' I said. 'It's not my fault. The man who brought me, put me here. And I'm not a foal. I'm four years old. I'm a grown-up horse. I don't want to argue.'

'Well,' she said, 'Of course, I don't want to argue with a young thing like you.'

I said no more.

In the afternoon, when she went out, Merrylegs told me all about her.

'The thing is,' said Merrylegs. 'Ginger's got a bad habit of biting. She used to bite **a lot**, and one day she bit Joe's arm.

After that, Miss Flora and Miss Jessie were afraid to come into the stable. They used to bring me nice things to eat, an apple or a carrot, but when Ginger was in that stall, they didn't come. I hope they will come again now.'

'Why does she bite?' I asked.

'She says people have never been kind to her,' said Merrylegs. 'I think she was treated very badly before she came here. Everyone is kind here. I'm twelve years old, and I can tell you, there is not a better place for a horse than this.

John is the best groom. He has been here fourteen years, and he's very kind. It's Ginger's own fault that she did not stay in that stall.'

# Chapter 5
# A Good Start

The next morning, John took me into the yard and gave me a good *grooming. Then, just as I was going into my stall, Squire Gordon came to look at me. He looked pleased.

'John,' he said, 'I'd like to ride the new horse tomorrow morning.'

'Yes, Sir,' said John.

The next day, my master rode me. I remembered my mother's advice, and I tried to do exactly what he wanted me to do. He was a very good rider, and thoughtful for his horse, too. When he came home, his wife was at the hall door.

grooming: brushing a horse

'Do you like him?' she asked.

'He's lovely,' he replied. 'What shall we call him?'

'What about Ebony?' she said. 'He's as black as ebony.'

'No, not Ebony.'

'What about Blackbird, like your uncle's old horse?'

'No, he is much handsomer than old Blackbird.'

'Yes,' she said, 'He's a beauty, and he's got such a sweet, good-tempered face, and such lovely, *intelligent eyes – Shall we call him Black Beauty?'

'**Black Beauty** – yes, that's perfect,' said the Squire.

And so, it was.

Back in the stables, Joe, the stable boy said to John, 'I'd call him Rob Roy. I never saw two horses more alike. But that would bring back bad memories.'

intelligent: clever

'Well,' said John. 'They're brothers. Farmer Grey's old Duchess was the mother of them both.'

I didn't know that. Poor Rob Roy who was killed at that hunt was my brother! No wonder my mother was so upset.

John was very proud of me, and he talked to me a lot. Of course, I didn't understand everything, but I learnt to know what he wanted me to do. I grew very fond of him. He was so gentle and kind. He seemed to know just how a horse feels. When he brushed my head, he went as carefully over my eyes as if they were his own.

Joe was just as gentle, so I was happy.

A few days after this, I had to go out with Ginger in the carriage. She behaved very well. When we came to a hill, instead of slowing her *pace, she pulled harder. John never had to use the *whip with either of us. We worked well together.

---

pace: how fast you go
whip: a long thin piece of leather people use to make the horse go faster

---

After we had been out two or three times together, we became quite friendly, and I began to feel very much at home.

As for Merrylegs, he and I soon became great friends. He was such a cheerful, brave, good-tempered, little pony that he was a favourite with everyone, and especially the two girls, Miss Jessie and Flora. They used to ride him around the orchard.

# Chapter 6
## Freedom

I was happy in my new place. I had a light airy stable and the best food. What more could I want? Freedom, of course! I missed it. Week after week, month after month, I had to stand up in a stable or work.

Now, I'm not complaining, because I know it must be so. I just want to say that, it is hard for a young horse.

Sometimes, when John took me out to exercise, I jumped or danced, and shook my head. He was always good and *patient.

'Steady my boy,' he said. 'Wait a bit, and we'll have a good ride.'

Then as soon as we were out of the village, he gave me a fast trot and I was happy.

patient: able to wait calmly for something

Sometimes we had our freedom for a few
hours. This used to be on sunny Sundays in the
summertime. The carriage never went out on
Sundays.

It was a great treat to be put in the paddock
or the old orchard; the grass was so cool and
soft to our feet, and we had the freedom to do as
we liked – to gallop, to lie down, and roll over
on our backs, or to eat the grass.

It was a very good time for talking, and we
used to stand together by a cherry tree and chat.

# Chapter 7
# Ginger

One day, when Ginger and I were standing alone in the shade, we had a long chat.

She asked me about my breaking in, and I told her.

'Well,' she said, 'you were very lucky. My experience was very different. **Nobody**, horse or man, was kind to me. I was taken from my mother when I was very young, and there was no kind master to look after me.

'My old master, Mr Ryder – he was kind; but he gave all the hard work to his son. His son was a strong, tall man. They called him Samson, and he used to *boast that no horse could throw him off. He was a cruel, hard man. He had a hard voice, a hard heart and a hard hand. He wanted me to be a quiet, *obedient horse.'

Ginger *stamped her foot as if the very thought of him made her angry.

---

boast: to talk proudly about something
obedient: always doing as people tell you to do
stamp: to put your foot down hard when you are angry

'If I did not do what he wanted, he got angry. One morning, he came for me early, and ran me round for a long time. Then, he brought a saddle and bridle and a new kind of bit.

The new bit was very *painful, and I *reared up suddenly. This made him angrier, and he began to whip me. I began to kick and rear, and we had a fight. I wanted to get him off.

rear up

At last, after a terrible *struggle, I threw him off backwards.

I heard him fall heavily on the ground. Then, I galloped off to the other end of the field. There, I turned round, and I saw him slowly getting up and going into the stable. I stood under a tree and watched, but nobody came to catch me.

painful: hurting a lot
struggle: a fight

The sun was very hot. I wanted to lie down and rest, but the saddle was still on, so it was very uncomfortable, and there was no water to drink.

I saw the other foals led in to the stable, and I knew they were having some food.

'At last, I saw the old master come out with a bowl in his hand. His voice was clear and kind. He came slowly, shaking the oats about in the bowl, and speaking *cheerfully and gently to me. 'Come along, *lassie, come along.'

I stood still and let him come up. He held the oats for me, and I began to eat. His voice took all my fear away. He stood by, patting and stroking me while I was eating. When he saw the blood on my side he was very upset. 'Poor, lassie!' he said. Then, he quietly led me to the stable. Samson stood at the door. I laid my ears back and *snapped at him. 'Keep out of her way,' said the master.

'She's a dangerous animal,' said Samson.

'A bad-tempered man will **never** make a good-tempered horse,' replied his father.

---

cheerfully: happily
lassie: an affectionate term for a female
snap: to try and bite

Then, he led me into my stall, took off the saddle and bridle, and tied me up. He called for a bucket of warm water and a *sponge. Then, he took off his coat, and he sponged my sides gently. '**Whoa**! my *pretty one,' he said. 'Stand still, stand still.' His kind voice made me feel better. The skin was so broken at the corners of my mouth, I could not eat the *hay. He told the man to fetch a good *bran mash. That mash was soft and *healing to my mouth.

The next time that Ginger and I were together in the paddock, she told me about her first place.

'After my breaking in,' she said, 'I was sold to a fashionable gentleman, and I was sent to London.

In this place, we were reined very tightly. The coachman and the master thought we looked more *stylish like that. It was awful.

sponge: a soft thing to wash with
pretty: beautiful
hay: dry grass that horses eat and sleep on
bran mash: a soft food to eat because her mouth was hurt
healing: making something better
stylish: fashionable, elegant

It made my neck ache, and the bit was sharp. It hurt my tongue and my mouth. It was worst when we had to stand for hours waiting for our mistress at some grand party or event. If I stamped with *impatience, I was whipped. It was terrible.'

'Didn't your master think about you?' I said.

'No,' said Ginger. 'He wanted a stylish horse and carriage. That was all. I don't think he knew a lot about horses.

'I was ready to work hard, but they made me angry. They had no right to make me *suffer like that.

'I grew more and more bad-tempered. I couldn't help it. And I began to bite and kick when anyone came to *harness me. Then, the groom hit me, and one day, when they were pulling my head up with that *rein, I began to kick with all my strength. I soon broke free, and that was the end of that place.

---

impatience: not wanting to wait for something
suffer: to have a hard time, feel bad
harness: to put on all the pieces to fasten a horse to a carriage (rein, bit, bridle)
rein: When you ride a horse, you hold the reins and you can stop or guide it by pulling on the reins.

I came here not long before you did. I *made up my mind** that men were my enemies.

Of course, it is very different here, but who knows how long it will last?'

'Well,' I said, 'I don't think you should bite or kick John or Joe.'

'I won't,' said Ginger, 'while they are good to me.'

I noticed that as the weeks went by, Ginger became more gentle and cheerful. And one day, Joe said, 'I think that mare is getting fond of me.'

'Kindness is all she wants, poor thing!' said John.

Master noticed the change, too, and one day when he got out of the carriage and came to speak to us, he stroked her beautiful neck. 'Well, my pretty one. How are you now? You're a lot happier than when you came to us, I think.'

She put her nose up to him in a friendly, *trustful way**, and he stroked it gently.

made up your mind: to decide
trustful: (here) knowing someone will not hurt you

# Chapter 8
## Merrylegs

The vicar, had a large family of boys and girls. Sometimes they used to come and play with Jessie and Flora. One of the girls was as old as Jessie. Two of the boys were older, and there were several little ones.

When they came, there was a lot of work for Merrylegs, because they loved riding him.

One afternoon, he was out with them for a long time, and when Joe brought him in, he said, 'There, now behave yourself, or we'll *get into trouble.'

'What did you do, Merrylegs?' I asked.

'Oh!' he said, with a shake of his little head, 'I gave those young people a lesson. They did not understand that I was tired, so I just *tipped them off backwards. That was the only thing, they could understand.'

> get into trouble: to do something bad so that someone is angry with you
> tip: (here) to go onto his back legs and let the boy slide off

'What!' I said. 'You threw the children off? You **never** do that! Did you throw Jessie or Flora?'

He looked very *offended, and said, 'Of course not. I would never do that. I'm their best friend and their riding-teacher. It wasn't them, it was the boys,' he said, shaking his mane, 'They must learn as we learnt when we were foals.

The girls rode me for nearly two hours, and then the boys thought it was their turn. I was nice. They took turns to ride me, and I galloped them about, up and down the fields for a good hour. They each had a big stick for a riding-whip, and they hit me too hard with them. I let them play for a while. Then, I thought, 'That's enough, now.' So I stopped two or three times, as a *hint.

'Boys think a pony is like a train. They never think that a pony can get tired, or have any feelings. So, when one was whipping me, I just rose up on my *hind legs and let him *slip off behind. That was all.

---

offended: sad that someone should think that
hint: a sign, a suggestion
hind: back
slip off: fall gently to the ground

'He got on again, and I did the same.

'They aren't bad boys. They don't want to be cruel. I like them very much, but I had to give them a lesson.

'When they brought me to Joe and told him, I think he was very angry to see such big sticks.'

'Those boys *deserved a good kick,' said Ginger.

'Yes,' said Merrylegs, 'But I won't forget all the kindness I've had here. No! Good places make good horses. I love our people, and I don't want to *upset them,' said Merrylegs.

'If I start kicking, I'll be sold. I don't want to work at a seaside town, giving children rides along the beach all day. No,' he said, shaking his head, 'I don't want that.'

The longer I lived at Birtwick, the happier I felt. Our master and mistress were loved by everyone. They were good and kind to everyone; not only men and women, but horses and ponies, dogs and cats, cows and sheep and birds, too.

> deserve: to get what is right for you
> (a reward or a punishment)
> upset: to make somebody unhappy

# Chapter 9
# A Stormy Day

One autumn day, my master had to go on business. It was raining heavily, and it was very windy. We rode along happily till we came to the low wooden bridge.

'Come back as soon as you can,' said the man at the *toll gate. 'The river is rising fast.'

We got to the town, but it was late afternoon before we started the journey home. 'I've never been out in such a bad storm,' said my master, and he patted me.

We rode along the side of a *wood, and the branches of the trees *swayed about in the wind.

toll gate: a gate where you pay
money to go across a bridge
wood: a small forest
sway: to move from side to side

'I wish we were away from this wood,' said my master. 'It's very dangerous. A tree could fall on us.'

The words were hardly out of his mouth when there was a loud crack and a huge tree fell across the road, just in front of us. I was frightened, so I stopped. My master jumped down, and he was at my head in a moment.

'That was close,' he said.

We continued on, but by the time we got to the bridge it was late. We could see that the river water was very high. That happened sometimes, so my master did not stop. However, the moment my feet touched the first part of the bridge, I knew there was something wrong. I stopped.

'Go on, Beauty,' said my master, but I didn't move.

'What's the matter, Beauty?' he said.

Of course, I could not tell him, but I knew that the bridge was not safe.

Just then the man at the toll-gate on the other side ran out of the house.

'**Stop! Hello! Stop!**' he cried.

'What's the matter?' shouted my master.

'The bridge is broken in the middle, and part of it has gone. If you ride on to it, you'll fall into the river.'

'**You Beauty**!' said Squire Gordon, and he took the bridle and gently turned me round. We went along the road by the river side.

The wind wasn't so strong now. I trotted quietly along. Then, my master said in a serious voice, 'You saved my life, Black Beauty. We nearly *drowned.'

At last, we came to the park gates. The gardener was waiting for us. 'Mrs Gordon has been very worried,' he said.

We saw a light at the hall door and at an upstairs window. Mrs Gordon ran out, saying, 'Oh, you're safe! Oh, I've been so worried. I imagined all kinds of things. Did you have an accident?'

'No, my dear, your Black Beauty saved my life. The wooden bridge was broken. We nearly drowned.'

'Animals have much better senses than we do,' she said. 'They often save people's lives.'

I heard no more, as they went into the house, and John took me to the stable.

Oh, what a good supper he gave me that night – and a lovely, thick bed of *straw! I was glad of that, because I was very tired.

drown: to die under the water

straw:

# Chapter 10
## The Sad Goodbye

I lived in this happy place for three years, then something sad happened. We heard that Mrs Gordon was ill. The doctor was often at the house, and the master looked unhappy. Then, we heard that she had to leave her home, and go to a warm country for two or three years. We were all unhappy.

John went about his work silent and sad, and Joe looked sad, too.

There was a lot of coming and going and Ginger and I had a lot of work.

First, Miss Jessie and Flora left. They came to say goodbye, and they *hugged Merrylegs like an old friend.

The master sold Ginger and me to a friend of his. He gave Merrylegs to the vicar, who wanted a pony for his wife. Joe was employed to look after him and to help in the house. I thought that Merrylegs was very lucky.

> hug: to put your arms around someone to show love

The evening before he left, Squire Gordon came into the stable to give his horses a last pat. He was very sad. I knew that by his voice.

John took us to Earlshall Park. It was a large house with a lot of stables. We were taken to a lovely stable, and put in stalls next to each other.

Half an hour later, John and our new groom, Mr York came in to see us.

'Now, John,' said Mr York, tell me about these horses.'

'Well,' said John, 'The black one has the most perfect temper. I think, he's always been treated with kindness. But Ginger has been treated badly. She used to bite and kick when she came to us. Then, after a few months she was fine with us. If she is well-treated, she behaves well. You have to treat her well.'

'Of course,' said York.

They were going out of the stable, when John stopped and said, 'We've never used the *check-rein with them.'

> check-rein: a short rein to make
> the horse's head go higher –
> it's very uncomfortable for the horse.

'Well,' said York, 'they must wear the check-rein here. Lady Elizabeth likes her *carriage horses to look stylish.'

'I'm sorry to hear that,' said John. 'Well, I must go now, or I'll miss the train.'

He came round to each of us and gave us a pat. I held my face close to him; that was all I could do to say goodbye; and then he left, and I haven't seen him since.

The next day, we were led round to the front of the house.

Soon, Lady Elizabeth came outside. She walked round to look at us. She was a tall, proud-looking woman.

'York,' she said, 'you must put those horses' heads higher. I can't have my horses looking like this.

carriage

'Yes, my lady,' said York. He got down from the carriage and came round to our heads. Then, he *shortened the rein. That day, we had a steep hill to go up, and I understood why horses hated this check-rein.

One day, my lady came down later than usual.

'Get those horses' heads up, York.' she said.

York came to me first, while the groom stood at Ginger's head. He pulled my head back and fixed the rein. It was very uncomfortable.

Then, he went to Ginger. The moment York took hold of the rein, she reared up so suddenly that she hit York's nose hard and knocked his hat off. The groom nearly fell to the ground.

At once they both flew to her head; but she went on rearing and kicking. Finally, she kicked the carriage over and fell down. She kicked me, too.

The groom quickly set me free from Ginger and the carriage, and led me to my stall. He left me in the check-rein which was very uncomfortable.

shorten: to make shorter

Soon, Ginger was led into the stable by two grooms. York came with her and gave his orders, and then came to look at me. Quickly, he took off the check-rein.

'I hate these check-reins!' he said. 'Horses hate them, too.'

Ginger was never put into the carriage again, but when she was well again, one of Lady Elizabeth's younger sons said he'd like to have her. As for me, I still had to go in the carriage.

I can't describe how I suffered with that check-rein. It was awful.

# Chapter 11
# Lady Anne and the Runaway Horse

Early in the spring, Lady Elizabeth and some of her family went up to London. I was left at home with Ginger and some other horses.

Her daughter, Lady Anne stayed at the hall. She loved riding on horseback and she was a very good horsewoman. She was kind and she was also beautiful. She chose me for her horse, and called me Black Auster. I enjoyed these rides very much. Sometimes Ginger came with us, and sometimes Lizzie.

Lizzie was a pretty golden mare with a lovely white mane. Ginger, who knew her better than I did, told me she was nervous.

Lady Anne's cousin, Blantyre was staying at the hall. He always rode Lizzie, and he praised her so much that one day Lady Anne decided to ride her.

When we came to the door, Blantyre looked *worried.

> worried: nervous

'What's going on?' he said. 'Are you tired of Black Auster?'

'No, of course not,' she replied, 'but I'd like to ride your lovely horse, Lizzie. You're always saying how wonderful she is. And she looks like a lady's horse.'

'I don't think you should ride her,' he said. 'She is lovely, but she's too nervous for you to ride. She's not safe.'

'My dear cousin,' said Lady Anne, laughing, 'please don't worry about me. I've been a horsewoman since I was a baby. So please help me onto the saddle.'

Blantyre helped her onto the saddle, and gave her the reins, and then he got on me.

Just as we were moving off, somebody came with a message from Lady Harriet. 'Could you ask Dr Ashley this question for her, and bring the answer?' he said.

The village was about a kilometre away. We went along happily until we came to the doctor's house.

Blantyre got down at the gate, and was going to open it for Lady Anne, but she said, 'I'll wait for you here, and you can hang Auster's rein on the gate.'

'I won't be five minutes,' he said.

'Don't worry,' she said. 'Lizzie and I won't run away.'

He hung my rein on the gate and walked up to the house. Lizzie was standing quietly by the side of the road with her back to me. Lady Anne was *humming a little song. There was a field on the opposite side of the road, and the gate was open. Just then, several young foals trotted towards us. There was a boy with them.

The foals were wild and playful, and one of them *bumped into Lizzie. She galloped off.

I gave a loud neigh for help. Blantyre heard and he came running to the gate. He saw Lizzie in the distance.

Quickly, he jumped into the saddle, and we galloped after them. Lizzie suddenly disappeared. We rode on.

An old man was walking by the road. 'She's gone to the *heath, Sir,' he shouted. I knew this heath very well. The ground was very rough. It was the worst place for a gallop.

hum: to sing without words
bump into: to hit
heath: an area of open land, not farmland

When we reached the heath, we saw Lady Anne's green jacket flying on before us. Her hat was gone, and her long brown hair was streaming behind her.

About halfway across the heath there was a wide *ditch. 'This will stop them!' I thought. But no; Lizzie jumped and fell.

Blantyre groaned, 'Now, Auster, do your best!' I prepared myself, and with one leap, I jumped over the ditch.

Poor Lady Anne lay on the ground. Blantyre kneeled down and called her name. There was no sound. Her face was white and her eyes were closed. 'Annie, dear Annie, please speak!' he cried. But there was no answer. He felt her wrist, then jumped up and looked round for help.

Two men saw Lizzie running wild without a rider, and they came to help.

'What can I do?' asked the first man.

'Can you ride?'

No, not very well, but I want to help Lady Anne. She was very good to my wife this winter.'

'Then take this horse and ride to the doctor's house. Ask him to come immediately. Then, go to the hall. Tell them to send me the carriage, with Lady Anne's maid. I'll stay here.'

'All right, Sir, I'll do my best.'

He then got into the saddle, and I took him to the doctor's. Then, we went to the hall.

Ginger was saddled and sent off to get Anne's brother, Lord James.

It seemed a long time before Ginger came back, and before we were left alone.

'I can't tell you much,' she said. 'I heard the doctor say, 'She's not dead.' They put her in the carriage, and we came home together. I heard Lord James say to a gentleman, that no bones were broken, and that she has not spoken yet.'

Two days after the accident, Blantyre visited with Lord James. He patted me and said, 'Good horse. Well done.'

'I'm sure Black Auster knew of Annie's danger,' he told Lord James. 'She shouldn't ride any other horse.' I learnt from their conversation that Lady Anne was better.

'She'll soon be able to ride again,' said Lord James.

This was good news because I loved her.

> ditch: a channel in the ground to carry water away

# Chapter 12
# Robert Smith

Now I must tell you a little about Robert Smith. He was gentle and very good with horses. He could doctor them as well as a vet, and he was a very good driver. He was a handsome man, and he was clever, too. I think everybody liked him; certainly, the horses did. However, he had one big fault, and that was his love of drink.

Robert promised not to drink, and he kept his promise. So, York trusted him to manage the stables while he was in London with the family.

It was early in April. Blantyre had to return to the army, and Robert drove him to the train station in the carriage. I was chosen for the journey.

At the station, Blantyre gave Robert some money and said goodbye. 'Take care of Lady Anne, Robert, and keep Black Auster for her to ride.'

We left the carriage at the maker's workshop to be painted, and then Robert rode me to the White Lion Inn.

He ordered the *hostler to feed me well, and have me ready for him at four o'clock. A nail in one of my front hooves was coming *loose, and the hostler noticed it.

When Robert came into the yard at five, he said, 'I won't leave till six, as I've met some old friends.' The hostler then told him about the nail. 'Shall I look at the shoe?' he asked.

'No,' said Robert, 'it will be all right till we get home.'

He spoke in a very loud voice, and I was surprised that he did not fix the shoe. He was usually very careful about our shoes. When he finally came for me at nine o'clock, he was in a very bad temper.

He made me gallop out of the town. The roads were stony, and my shoe became looser. Then, as we got near to the toll gate, my shoe came off. Robert didn't notice.

After the toll-gate, there was a long road, covered with stones – large sharp stones. I had to gallop at top speed. It was very painful.

---

hostler: a man employed to look after horses at an inn
loose: coming out, not fixed in place

I fell down hard on both my knees. Robert fell off.

I soon got up on my feet again, and I *limped to the side of the road. The moon was in the sky, and by its light, I could see Robert Smith lying on the ground. He did not get up.

Robert did not move. I could do nothing for him. I listened for the sound of horses or footsteps! The road was quiet. I stood watching and listening.

It was nearly midnight when I heard the sound of a horse's feet.

I neighed loudly, and was very happy to hear an answering neigh from Ginger and men's voices. They came slowly over the stones, and stopped by Robert.

Joe jumped out. 'It's Robert,' he said, 'and he isn't moving!'

Ned followed. 'He's dead,' he said.

Then, they came and looked at me. They soon saw my cut knees.

'Look! The horse has thrown him!' said Ned. 'That's strange. Black Auster is always very good-tempered.'

Joe then tried to lead me forward. I took a step, but almost fell again. 'He's got a bad foot as well as his knees,' said Joe. 'Look at his hoof. That's why he fell down, poor horse! Why did Robert ride a horse over these stones without a shoe?'

'I'm afraid it's the old problem again,' said Ned. What should we do?'

Then, they had a conversation, and they agreed that Joe should lead me, and that Ned should take the body.

Ginger stood as still as a stone, while they got the body onto the cart.

> limp: to walk with difficulty because your leg or foot is hurt

I shall never forget that walk home. It was more than six kilometres, and I was in great pain. Joe was very kind to me.

At last, I reached my stall, and had some oats; and after that Joe *wrapped my knees in wet cloths, and cleaned my foot. Then, I lay down on the straw and slept.

The foot and knees took a long time to heal and they were very painful. They put something on the front of both knees to take all the hair off. They had a reason for this.

The landlord and the groom at the White Lion told my master that Robert was drunk when he left the inn. The man at the toll-gate said he galloped through the gate; and my shoe was found on the road. It was clear that the accident was not my fault.

Everybody felt sorry for Robert's wife, Susan. She kept saying, 'He was a good man! It was the drink. Why do they sell it?'

She and her six children had to leave their lovely home, and go to that big, gloomy *workhouse.

wrap: to cover, put round and round
workhouse: a place people went when they had no money or home

I was put into a small field and left there for a month or two. There were no other animals there, and though I enjoyed the freedom and the sweet grass, I felt very lonely. Ginger and I were good friends, and now I missed her. Then, one morning the gate was opened, and Ginger trotted in.

With a happy neigh, I trotted up to her. 'Why are you here?' I asked her.

'It's a long story,' she said. 'But now, I need to rest and get better.'

Soon after I left the stable, there was a race, and Lord James wanted to ride Ginger. On the day of the race, he made Ginger keep up with the riders at the front. She tried her hardest, and she came in with the first three horses. However, he was too heavy for her, and her back was badly hurt.

We did not gallop about, but we ate together and lay down together. We stood for hours, with our heads together, talking. We passed our time like this until the family returned from London.

One day, we saw the Earl come into the field, and York was with him. The Earl was very angry.

'My old friend, trusted me to give a good home to these two horses, and now both are hurt. Ginger can stay and rest in the field for twelve months. But I must sell Black Auster. I can't have knees like these in my stables.'

# Chapter 13
# A London Cab Horse

I was lucky, I was sold to a London cab driver called Jeremiah Barker. But as everyone called him Jerry, I shall do the same.

Polly, his wife, was a plump, little woman, with dark hair, dark eyes, and a happy smile. They had a lovely little boy called Harry and a lovely little girl called Dolly. They were the happiest family I have ever known.

On the first morning, when I was well-groomed, Polly and Dolly came into the yard to see me and make friends. Harry was there too, helping his father. Polly brought me a slice of apple, and Dolly a piece of bread.

I felt like the Black Beauty of the old days. I let them see that I wanted to be friendly. Polly thought I was very handsome, and too good for a cab, if I didn't have the broken knees.

'I don't know whose fault that was,' said Jerry. 'Shall we call him Jack, after the old horse?'

'Yes,' said Polly. 'It's a good name for a horse.'

The first week of my life as a cab horse was very tiring. I wasn't used to London, and the noise. The crowds of horses, carts, and carriages that I had to make my way through, made me feel nervous. However, I soon found that I could trust my driver, and then I relaxed and got used to it.

Jerry was a good driver, and he cared about his horses. In a short time, Jerry and I understood each other as well as horse and man can do.

# Chapter 14
## Poor Ginger

One day, while our cab was waiting outside one of the parks, an old cab drove up beside ours.

The horse was an old *worn-out chestnut, with a badly groomed coat, and bones that showed through it.

I was eating some hay, and the wind rolled some her way. The poor horse stretched out her long thin neck and picked it up. Then, she turned and looked about for more. There was a *hopeless look in the *dull eye. 'Where have I seen this horse before?' I wondered. Then, she looked at me and said, 'Black Beauty, is that you?'

worn-out: made very tired by hard work
hopeless: having no hope
dull: not shiny, (here) unhappy

It was Ginger! But she looked very different! The face and the eyes that were once so full of life, were now full of suffering.

Our drivers were standing together, so I walked up to her, so that we could talk.

It was a sad *tale that she told me.

> tale: a story

After twelve months' rest at Earls Hall, she was ready for work again, and she was sold to a gentleman.

She was sold several times after that, and each new job was worse than the last.

'And so, at last,' she said, 'I was bought by a man who keeps several cabs and horses, and rents them out. Sadly, he is very unkind and he treats his horses very badly. You look well. I'm happy about that. My life has been awful.'

They know I'm ill, and that this will be my last job. They whip me and work me hard. They never think about me. They paid for me, and must *get their money's worth. I don't even have a holiday on Sunday.'

'That's awful. Jerry and I never work on Sunday,' I said.

'You're lucky. You've got a good master.'

'But you always used to *stand up for yourself. What happened?'

'Yes, I did!' said Ginger, 'But it's no use. Men are stronger than us. If they are cruel and have no feelings, there is nothing that we can do. I wish I was dead.

'I've seen dead horses, and I'm sure they don't feel any pain. I want to *drop down dead at my work.'

---

get your money's worth: to get good value from something you've paid for
stand up for yourself: not let people treat you badly
drop down dead: to die quickly, where you are

---

I was very upset, and I put my nose up to hers, but I couldn't say anything to *comfort her.

I think she was pleased to see me, because she said, 'You're the only friend I ever had.'

Just then her driver came up, and with a *tug at her mouth, he drove off. I felt very sad.

A few days after this, a cart with a dead horse in it passed our cab stand. The head hung out of the back of the cart. It was a chestnut horse with a long, thin neck. I saw a white mark on the forehead. I think it was Ginger.

I hope it was, because then her troubles were *over. She was not suffering any more.

Soon after that, Jerry stopped working as a cab driver. He went to live in the country with Polly and the children, and he sold me.

comfort: to make someone feel happier
tug: a hard pull
over: finished

# Chapter 15
# The Farmer and his Grandson

At the sale, of course, I was put with the old broken-down horses. I was very nervous because I wanted a good home!

Then, I noticed a man who looked like farmer. He had a kind face, and he was with a little boy.

When the farmer came up to us, he stood still and gave us a sad look. I saw him look at me, and I looked back at him. I still had a good mane and tail.

'There's a horse, Davie, that has known better days,' he said.

'Poor old horse!' said the boy.

The farmer gave me a kind pat on the neck. I put out my nose in answer to his kindness. The boy stroked my face.

'Look, Grandpa. He understands kindness. Can't you buy him and make him young again? You helped Ladybird.'

'I can't make all old horses young. Ladybird wasn't very old,' said the farmer.

'But, Grandpa, I don't believe that this one is old. Look at his mane and tail.'

The farmer laughed. 'Bless you! You're as *horsey as your old grandfather.'

'Please buy him, Grandpa.'

The man who brought me to the sale now spoke. 'You're right young man. He's not old. He's just tired out from hard work. He's a lovely, gentle horse. Give him a chance. You can have him for five pounds.'

'Oh, Grandpa, please buy him,' said the little boy.

'Go on, then. I'll take him,' said the farmer.

The boy smiled happily. He was *delighted.

My new home was a large field with a stable.

'Now, you, Davie, must look after him. He's yours,' said the farmer to his grandson.

> horsey: someone who knows about horses and likes them
> delighted: very happy

Davie was proud of his horse. He came to see me every day. He usually gave me a carrot, or something good. He always came with kind words, and I grew very fond of him. Sometimes he brought his grandfather to see me. He always looked at my legs.

'He's improving. I think he'll be better in the spring.'

With the rest, the good food, and gentle exercise, I soon began to feel better.

Then, in March, the farmer tried me in a carriage. My legs were not stiff now, and it was easy for me to pull the carriage. I was happy.

'He's growing younger,' said Davie. 'I'm so glad you bought him!'

'So am I, but he has to thank **you** more than me. We must find him a nice place to live and owners who will be kind to him.'

# Chapter 16
# My Last Home

One day, the groom brushed my mane and my coat very carefully. Davie seemed half-nervous and half-happy when he got in the cart with his grandfather.

'If the ladies like him,' said Davie's grandfather, 'they'll be very kind to him and he'll have a good home. We can only try.'

A kilometre or two from the village, we came to a pretty, little house. Davie rang the bell, and asked if Miss Kate or Miss Ellie were at home. Yes, they were. So, Davie stayed with me, and his grandfather went into the house.

In about ten minutes, he returned, followed by two ladies. One was a tall lady, with blonde hair and blue eyes. Her name was Ellie. The other was a younger lady, with dark hair and brown eyes and a happy face. Her name was Kate. They came and looked at me and asked questions.

The younger lady, Kate liked me very much. 'He's got such a lovely face. He's **beautiful**,' she said.

'I'm worried because he's fallen before,' said Ellie.

'Many good horses have broken knees because their drivers were careless. It's not the horse's fault,' said the farmer.

In spite of the broken knees, Miss Ellie wanted me. 'We'd love to have him,' she said, smiling.

I was led into a comfortable stable, fed, and left to myself.

The next day, when the groom was cleaning my face, he said, 'You've got a star just like the star that Black Beauty had. You're the same height, too. I wonder where Black Beauty is now.'

Then, he began to look carefully at me.

'A white star on the forehead, and one white foot. You **must** be Black Beauty! Beauty do you remember me? I'm little Joe Green – the stable boy.' And he began patting me.

I could not remember him, because he was an adult now, with a black beard and a man's voice.

I put my nose up to him, and tried to say that we were friends. I never saw a man so pleased.

'I wonder who broke your knees, my old Beauty! You've been badly treated somewhere. I'll make sure you have a happy life now. I wish John Manly was here to see you.'

In the afternoon I was put into a small carriage and brought to the door. Ellie was going to try me with Joe. She was a good driver, and she seemed pleased with me.

I heard Joe telling her about me. 'I'm sure he was Squire Gordon's old Black Beauty,' Joe said.

When we returned, Kate was waiting for her. Ellie told her all about me.

'I'll write to Mrs Gordon in Italy, and tell her that her favourite horse is here. She'll be very happy!' she said.

After this, they decided to call me Black Beauty.

I have now lived in this happy place a whole year. Joe is the best and kindest of grooms. My work is easy and pleasant, and I feel my strength and *spirits are all coming back again.

Davie always comes to see me when he can. My ladies have promised that they will **never** sell me, and so I have nothing to worry about.

> spirits: happiness, liveliness
> troubles: problems

So here my story ends. My *troubles are all over, and I am at home. Sometimes before I am properly awake, I think I am still in the orchard at Birtwick, standing under an apple tree.

# After reading

## Vocabulary

**1.** **Complete the puzzle.**

**Down**

1. the long hair on a horse's head
3. to run (horse)
4. a young horse

**Across**

7. a female horse
8. to talk (horse)
9. to walk (horse)

**2. Match the adjectives to their synonyms.**

1. pretty
2. cross
3. clever
4. handsome
5. hind
6. plump

a) intelligent
b) good-looking
c) back
d) beautiful
e) fat
f) angry

# Dictionary work

**1. Choose words from the box. Then, find another synonym in your dictionary.**

| tug | take care of | hug | groan |
|-----|--------------|-----|-------|

make a noise       ............, ............

look after       ............, ............

put your arms around............, ............

pull hard       ............, ............

**2. Now complete the sentences with the verbs from Activity 1. Use the past simple tense.**

1. The driver .......... at the reins and it hurt her mouth.
2. The two girls .......... Merrylegs when they said goodbye to him.
3. Jerry was very kind, and he .......... his horses.
4. The horse .......... because he was in pain.

# Language

1. **Complete the sentences with the verbs in the box.**

> stroke   suffer   drown   bite   praise   limp

1. Black Beauty's mother did not want him to ............... and kick.

2. Blantyre always ............... Lizzie and said nice things about her.

3. After Black Beauty fell and hurt his knees, he couldn't walk properly, so he ...............

4. Luckily, Black Beauty and his master didn't ............... in the river.

5. Horses ............... when they had to wear the check-rein. It was very painful.

6. Black Beauty's groom often patted and ............... him.

**2.** Complete the sentences with an everyday expression from the box.

> stylish    stand up for herself    bump into
> be too good for    get their money's worth

**1.** Black Beauty ............ Ginger in London when they were both pulling cabs.

**2.** Some people made their horses work hard because they wanted to ............ .

**3.** Polly thought that Black Beauty ............ a cab.

**4.** Black Beauty believed that Ginger was strong and she could ............ .

**5.** Lady Elizabeth wanted her horses to look ............ .

# Characters

**1.** Match the pictures to the texts and number the pictures.

## 1

Black Beauty has got a beautiful [1]black / white coat with a [2]black / white star on his forehead. He has got very [3]sad / intelligent eyes. Everybody loves him. He is very [4]bad-tempered / good-tempered and very [5]patient / impatient.

## 2

Ginger has got a beautiful [1]black / chestnut coat. She was [2]badly-treated / well-treated so she [3]bites / trots and kicks.

## 3

Merrylegs is a little [1]grey / white pony. He is [2]cheerful / noisy and [3]frightening / brave. The children loved to ride him. He was very [4]bad-tempered / good-tempered.

2. Which is your favourite horse and why? Write.

...................................................

...................................................

# Comprehension

1. **Write (T) True or (F) False.**

    **1.** Black Beauty lived on a farm with his
    mother until he was four years old.   T / F

    **2.** Black Beauty's brother was killed
    after a hunt.                          T / F

    **3.** Black Beauty did not like Ginger.   T / F

    **4.** Some of Ginger's owners were
    very cruel to her.                     T / F

    **5.** Squire Gordon sold Ginger and Black Beauty
    when he went to live abroad.           T / F

    **6.** After Black Beauty's back was hurt,
    his owner sold him to a cab driver
    in London.                             T / F

    **7.** Ginger was treated very badly by
    the owner of the cabs and she died.    T / F

    **8.** Black Beauty was very unhappy
    at his last home.                      T / F

# Speaking & Writing

## In pairs

1. **Discuss and make a poster.**

   Horses Have Feelings Too

   **These questions will help you:**

   *How are horses treated in your country?*
   *Do people feed the horses properly?*
   *Do they have a nice place to live?*
   *Do they carry heavy loads?*
   *What kind of work do they do?*
   *Are people kind to horses?*
   *What do horses like to eat?*

2. **What lessons do you learn from the story?**
   **Circle *Yes* or *No*.**

   1. Horses are intelligent animals and
      we need to treat them kindly.          Yes / No

   2. A bad-tempered man will never
      make a good-tempered horse.            Yes / No

   3. Horses don't have feelings.            Yes / No

3. **Do you like the story? Tick (✓).**

   ☐ I like the story. ❤
   ☐ I like the story very much. ❤ ❤
   ☐ I love the story. ❤ ❤ ❤